How to choose mushrooms?

How to easily recognize edible mushrooms in the woods!

Cristina & Olivier Rebière

HOW TO CHOOSE MUSHROOMS?

First edition. March 27, 2023.

Copyright © 2023 Cristina Rebiere.

ISBN: 979-8215532478

Written by Cristina Rebiere.

Table of Contents

We welcome you in your book *Nature Passion*: "**How to choose mushrooms?**" a practical guide, that we hope, will help you to easily recognize mushrooms but especially show you the joy of going out and picking them by yourself!

I love going out to pick mushrooms in the woods since I was a kid. When I was a child I asked my father whether a particular mushroom was edible or not. He did not know much either, and was was limited to only pick the ones he was sure they were edible. We were going to gather mushrooms every fall and it happened that we sometimes picked even tens of kilograms! We would then prepare preserves for winter. I have always dreamed of having a small atlas to help me recognize mushrooms :-)... Besides, if you already know our **Voyage Experience** books, this should not surprise you much since you already know that I am passionate about atlases;-). In our guides, I have sometimes put atlases of flowers, fruits or animals to help you recognize those you don't know when you're traveling far from home. This paper book is made after an eBook that you can have for free on your smartphone or Kindle (see at the end of the book how to do it) and where you can use all the features explained in the section: "How to use this eGuide ", and also contains a simplified navigation mode called "PhotoNav".

In this little guide, you will find pictures and edible mushrooms descriptions, but also places where you can find them. You can find at the end a section with gourmet recipes to delight you with the results of your mushrooms picking. This guide is not exhaustive and I have chosen the mushrooms you will mostly find in the woods. I preferred not to include those which are too similar to toxic mushrooms to avoid risks. In any case, the best advice I can give you is this one: **if you have any doubt about a fungus, better NOT pick it!**.

I will try to add others according to my findings and my wanderings...

DO YOU THINK MUSHROOM picking is not for you? Maybe you are not aware of all its advantages... The benefits of mushroom picking go beyond simple gluttony and I will give you some good reasons to get started ;-) :

- Walking in the woods keeps you **fit** because it is sport ... The advantage is that you do not even feel the effort since you will be concentrated on your quest ;-)
- It helps you to get some fresh air: there is no better place to get some fresh air as in the woods. Beyond the quality of the atmosphere you will enjoy other flavors and smells (*strong* pines' odor, *musky* hardwoods', *delicate* flowers' glades ... and even that of the fungi that you quickly become familiar...)
- You will enjoy the birds' songs - what sweet music to our ears that soothes and provides well-being without even noticing it!
- You will share moments and things with your family or friends... because mushroom picking is a constant wonder and a victory for every find!
- You will pass your knowledge: children love picking mushrooms! You probably think that this is not the case with yours because they are too connected to their computer or smartphone? Think again and try the experience! Perhaps you will be surprised by the result ... At all ages, children end up "caught in the game" especially if encouraged throughout the experience ;-) And then back home, they will be delighted eating their own discoveries ... So gourmet recipes within my special section will perhaps be helpful ;-)
- One last argument, although I think I could find some more:

you eat what you have picked and it makes you very proud, you'll see! In addition, you will know where your food comes from and how it was prepared, because it is you who will have made it!!!

For each mushroom, I will try to give you as many details as possible. If you have any doubt about the identity of a mushroom, it is best not to pick it! This will prevent digestive problems or worse ;-)... Some mushrooms are more tasteful than others, so I will use icons to indicate whether they are good or delicious, or if you should be careful...

 Delicious mushrooms!

Good mushrooms.

Please be careful because these mushrooms should be cooked, otherwise they are toxic

Identification characteristics

Here are some simple keys that will help you identify mushrooms you will encounter.

General form of thc fungus

The first thing you can identify is the general form of the fungus.

with a central stipe (foot)   **ball-shaped with a stipe**

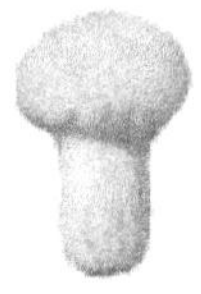

ball-shaped without a stipe

shaped as a bush

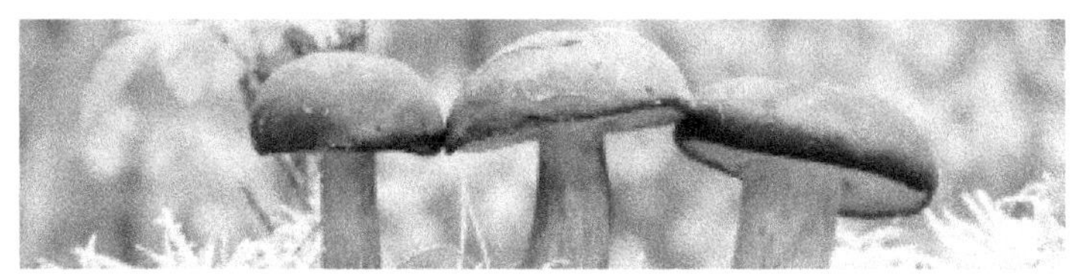

trumpet-shaped

club-shaped

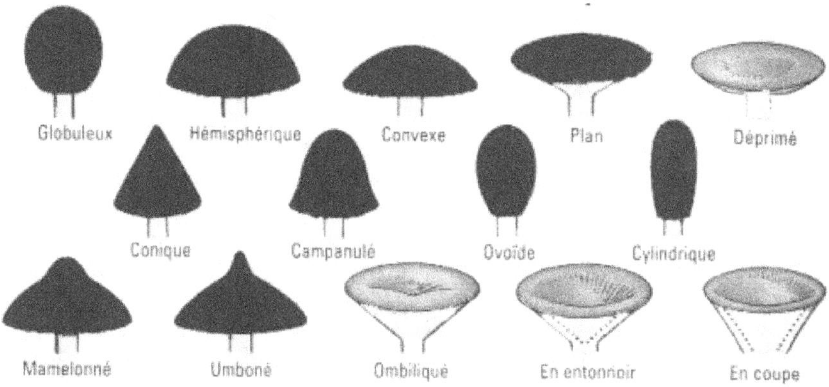

GENERAL SHAPE OF THE cap

1. Brown mushrooms

1.1 The russula

Russulas are among the most popular mushrooms in the woods and forests. They are part of the same genus as Lactarius, the difference between the two is that russulas do not produce a "milk" flow when broken.

Attention because only some russulas are edible! I suggest you pick just the ones you know or recognize without any doubt. 

The russulas do not usually have much taste.

You can either cook them in combination with other more flavorful mushrooms, or prepare them as a gratin with cheese to add flavor.

Bare-toothed Russula - *Russula vesca*

DESCRIPTION : the **cap** is pinkish to brown and often up to 15 cm wide. It often has protruding gills of the margin of white hat, quite soft and fragile. The **stipe** is white.

Edible russulas have a slight nutty flavor.

**Habitat and period of presence:**

These Russulas are very common in the forests of leafy and coniferous trees and begin to appear from May on. They persist until October.

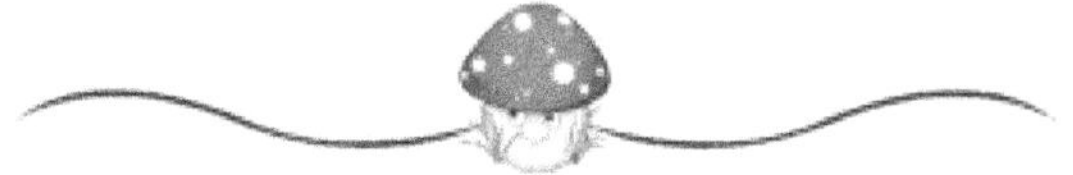

1.2 The "Boletus"

THIS TERM DESIGNATES several species of fungi. The *boletus* are characterized by tubes under the cap instead of blades. Boletus present the typical characteristics of fungi Boletales: young, they look like a "champagne cork" and adult, they have a convex figure with a cap, often thick. They all have a surface like a sponge under the cap, consisting of tubes.

Warning: some mushrooms are bitter, others can cause digestive problems, but they are rarely toxic.

One boletus can ruin a dish if it is of a bitter kind. So, if you have any doubts, try and taste a small piece of the cap and you will soon figure out if it is a bitter one.

Cep or **penny bun** - *Boletus edulis*

Photo 1.2 : Cep or penny bun

DESCRIPTION : the **cap** is convex from light brown to dark brown. Young, the cap is near the stipe, before flattening out at maturity. Its edges will raise and its stipe will swell. The **flesh** is white. The **hymenium** (=part which is under the cap) is, as with all boletus, under the form of firm and white tubes during the youth and colored in yellow, then olive green with age.

The **stipe** is white or yellowish, stubby at a young age and then becomes cylindrical.

The ceps are delicious and also have a nutty flavor.

Habitat and period of presence: The ceps can be found in leafy woods under beeches, oaks and chestnut trees. In coniferous woods they prefer spruces. They begin to appear in June and continue until November. They often grow in groups.

Pine bolete - *Boletus pinophilus*

Photo 1.3 : Pine bolete

DESCRIPTION : the **cap** is convex, has a garnet color to dark red-brown. In maturity its cap becomes "mushy". The **flesh** is white. The

hymenium has white and firms tubes for the young ones and turns to yellow, then olive green with age.

The **stipe** is red, stubby, measuring 70 to 150 mm long by 30 to 100 mm wide.

The ceps are delicious and also have a nutty flavor.

Habitat and period of presence: Pine boletes are usually in pine forests at altitude, but they are also present in mixed wood with leafy. They start appearing in July and persist until October. They often grow in small groups.

Dark cep - *Boletus aereus*

Photo 1.4 : Dark cep

DESCRIPTION: the **cap** is brown almost black and measure, when young, from 7 to 30 cm. The **flesh** is white and firm. The **hymeniumhas** white tubes, thin for the young, turning to yellow, then olive green with age.

The **stipe** is brown or ocher, stubby, measuring 6 to 10 mm.
The dark ceps are delicious and have a sweet flavor. Their flesh is crunchy.

**Habitat and period of presence**: The dark ceps are often found in the southern dry regions in the woods of leafy trees, preferring oaks. They begin to appear from August and persist until October.

Summer cep - *Boletus reticulatus* or *aestivalis*

Photo 1.5 : Summer cep

DESCRIPTION: the **cap** is reddish brown or ocher and never viscous. The **flesh** is white and firm. The **hymenium** has brown-olive tubes. The **stipe** is white, slightly reddish or light brown, potbellied, measuring 13 to 20 cm.

Summer ceps are delicious and have a sweet flavor.

Habitat and period of presence: Summer ceps are found in oak forests. They begin to appear from May on and continue through September.

Be careful not to confuse it with the **False cep** or **Bitter Bolete** - *Tylopilus felleus*. The difference is mainly in the color of the hymenium tubes that are pinkish for this boletus. It becomes even more bitter during cooking. It can cause digestive problems and even if it is not toxic, it is best to avoid it!

Photo 1.6 : FAUX Cèpe

BAY BOLETE - *Boletus badius*

Photo 1.7 : Bay bolete

DESCRIPTION: the **cap** is hemispherical before flattening out in maturity, its color is bay brown. It is velvety by dry weather but can become sticky when wet. The **flesh** is yellowish-white and firm. The **hymenium** has pale yellow or slightly greenish tubes, turning blue or black when touched. They go through the lemon yellow color with age.

The **stipe** is brownish yellow with the appearance of "wood".

The bay boletes are very good and have a sweet flavor.

Habitat and period of presence: The bay boletus are found in the forests of leafy or resinous trees. They appear especially during autumn.

Be careful because this mushroom can accumulate pollutants.

Royal bolete - *Boletus regius*

Photo 1.8 : Royal bolete

DESCRIPTION: the royal bolete looks like the summer cep, except that it has a pink-reddish cuticle (the thin skin covering the cap) and the stipe is pale yellow. The **cap** is hemispherical and convex with age, its color pinkish. It is velvety. The **flesh** is yellowish-white and firm. The **hymenium** has bright yellow tubes which turn to green with age.

The **stipe** is pale yellow, short and stocky, wide at the base.

The royal boletes are delicious and have a sweet flavor and smell.

Habitat and period of presence: The royal boletes are found in the forests of oaks and beeches, especially in southern regions. They appear from July to October.

Pay attention because it resembles to other boletus whose flesh turns blue, then you should do the test by taking a small piece.

Dotted stem bolete - *Boletus luridiformis ouerythropus*

Photo 1.9 : Dotted stem bolete

DESCRIPTION: The **cap** is hemispherical before flattening out in maturity, its color is dark brown with reddish-brown spots. The **flesh** is bright yellow, firm, turning quickly to blue when cut. The **hymeniumhas** yellow olive tubes which turns blue with age. The tubes are terminated with bright red-orange pores becoming blue, orange and yellow when touched.

The **stipe** is fibrous, yellow-orange with small bright red dots.

The Dotted stem bolete are delicious and have a sweet flavor and a fruity smell.

Please note that these mushrooms should be cooked (at least 15 minutes), otherwise they are toxic.

Habitat and period of presence: The Dotted stem bolete are found in the forests of oaks and conifers especially in small groups. They appear from July to November.

If you want to be sure to eliminate the risk of having any gastric problems, cut these boletes thinly to ensure proper cooking. The blue color of the flesh disappears with cooking.

Yellow Foot - *Craterellus lutescens*
or *Cantharellus lutescens*

Description: The **cap** is irregularly lobed, brown. The **flesh** is bright yellow, firm. The **hymenium** has bright colors of salmon pink color. The **stipe** is thin, yellow to orange.

The Yellow Foot is delicious and has a sweet flavor.

Habitat and period of presence: Yellow Foot can be found in coniferous forests especially in groups. They appear from July to November.

Photo 1.10 : Yellow Foot

VEINY CUP FUNGUS - *Disciotis venosa*

Photo 1.11 : Veiny cup fungus

DESCRIPTION: The **cap** is hemispherical, cup-shaped, and flatters with age with a deformed center, veined with a wavy margin. Its color is dark brown with yellowish white outside. The **flesh** is white-beige and exhales a bleach smell when broken. The **stipe** is very short (less than a centimeter), and anchors the cup to the ground.

The Veiny cup fungus have a good taste and a smell of bleach that disappears with cooking.

Please note that these mushrooms should be cooked (at least 15 minutes), otherwise they can cause digestive disorders.

Habitat and period of presence: The Veiny cup fungus can be found in the undergrowth of leafy forests, mainly ashes on calcareous soils. They appear in spring, from May to June.

If you find Veiny cup fungus it is quite possible that morels are also nearby as they grow in the same places.

Funnel Chanterelle - *Craterellus tubaeformis*

Photo 1.12 : Funnel Chanterelle

DESCRIPTION: Funnel Chanterelle are small mushrooms (3-12 cm) growing in groups on the moss and litter, often near rotten wood. The **cap** is convex on young fungi and later becomes depressed, then takes the form of a funnel with age. It is orange-brown. The **flesh** has an elastic consistency. The **hymenium** has yellow or silver gray gills, forked near the edges. The **stipe** is bright, yellow to orange, long, thin and hollow like a tube.

Funnel Chanterelles are very good mushrooms, especially fried or in soups, and are easily dried for preservation..

Habitat and period of presence: Funnel Chanterelles are found in wet places of leafy forests or mixed woodland. They grow in the fall until November. They grow in groups.

Poplar Mushroom - *Cyclocybe parasitica*
or *Agrocybe parasitica*

Photo 1.13 : Poplar Mushroom

DESCRIPTION: This is a gregarious mushroom that comes in groups of several specimens, whose stipes are soldered.

The **cap** is fleshy, globular, then convex and flatten with age. It is smooth and silky, brown to whitish. The **flesh** is white and firm. The **hymenium** consists of tight gills, beige becoming brown with age.

The **stipe** is firm and fibrous, pale yellow and ocher. It has a high wide silky ring white up to its stipe, becoming brown.

Poplar Mushrooms are very good and have a sweet flavor.

Habitat and period of presence: Poplar Mushrooms grow on dead wood and leafy stem (poplars) or willows. They begin to appear from May and continue until November. They grow in groups.

2. Yellow or orange mushrooms

G olden chanterelle - *Cantharellus cibarius*

Photo 2.1 : Golden chanterelle

DESCRIPTION: the **cap** is convex and flattened with age, funnelling in the middle, from 4 to 10 cm. The color is yellow and the margin is a little wound. The **flesh** is creamy white, thick and firm. The **hymenium** of the same color is constituted by lamelliform ridges. The **stipe** is of the same color, sometimes lighter from 4 to 7 cm high. It is fibrous.

The girolles are excellent edible mushrooms with a mild flavor and fruity smell.

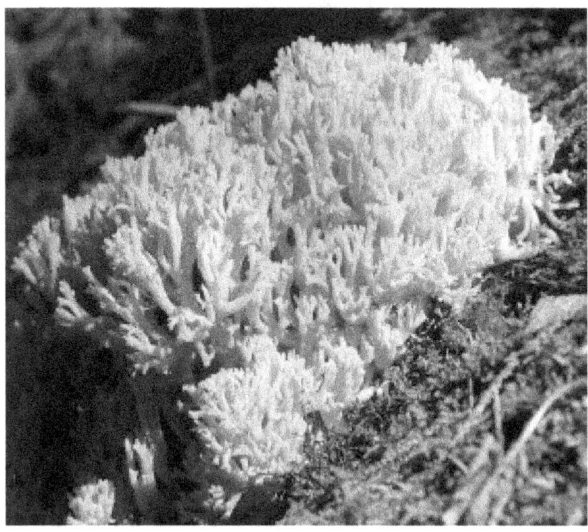

Habitat and period of presence: The girolles can be found in leafy (mainly birch or oak) and coniferous woods and start appearing in June and continue until October. They often grow in small groups.

Ramaria aurea

Photo 2.2 : Ramaria aurea

DESCRIPTION: it is a coral mushroom with numerous branches, cylindrical, upright and tight yellow. They are divided into small twigs denticulated atop. The **flesh** is white to yellowish.

The **stipe** is short and thick.

The ramaria are good and have a fruity flavor.

Habitat and period of presence: The ramaria aurea can be found in the undergrowth of leafy or coniferous trees, in humid places. They begin to appear from August and persist until October.

Cauliflower coral - *Ramaria botrytis*

Photo 2.3 : Cauliflower coral

DESCRIPTION: the aerial part, sometimes measuring up to 15 cm in diameter, looks like coral. The **sporophore** (organ producing spores) consists of a strong central stipe, dividing into a few roses ramuli dividing themselves in purple twigs, all like a cauliflower. Originally white, it passes like the stipe to pale yellow, becoming ocher or white. The **flesh** is white and firm.

The **stipe** is short court and thick..

Cauliflower corals are good and have a fruity flavor.

Habitat and period of presence: Cauliflower corals can be found in hardwoods especially beech. They begin to appear from August and persist until October.

Please be careful to not confuse these cauliflower corals with **beautiful clavaria** - *Ramaria Formosa* which are toxic . The difference is mostly in color - their ramuli are pink and yellow twigs whitish. The smell is unpleasant and taste bitter.

Photo 2.4 : Ramaria formosa NOT EDIBLE!!!

SHEATHED WOODTUFT - *Kuehneromyces mutabilis*

Photo 2.5 : Sheathed woodtuft

DESCRIPTION: This is a gregarious mushroom that comes in groups of several specimens whose stipes are welded. Strongly hygrophanous, it swells with water and changes its color.

The **cap** is hemispherical and becomes convex, then flattens with a slightly wavy margin and finely striated. It is yellowish, reddish-brown to the center. The **flesh** is soft. The **hymenium** is formed by tight gills, yellowish or cinnamon becoming rusty brown with age.

The **stipe** is yellowish up and brown down, no longer than 8 cm, often curved and fibrous. It is small, but quite stubborn. It has a slight membranous ring that disappears with age.

Sheathed woodtufts are delicious and have a sweet taste.

Habitat and period of presence: Sheathed woodtufts grow on dead wood and hardwood strains (beech or willows). They can also grow on spruces sometimes. They begin to appear from May and continue until November. They grow in groups.

Photo 2.6 : Galerina marginata NOT EDIBLE!!

BE CAREFUL NOT TO CONFUSE them with the *Galerina marginata* - to make a difference, remember that Sheathed woodtufts grow only in groups. Galerina marginata smells mealy.

Golden needle mushroom - *Flammulina velutipes*

Description: This is a gregarious mushroom that grows in large groups. The **cap** is small, 5-10 cm, viscous, yellow-orange to dark orange, darker in the center. The **flesh** is pale. The **hymenium** has thin pale gills for young mushrooms and becomes red with age. They are little tight. The **stipe** is velvety, dark reddish brown to blackish towards the base.

Golden needle mushrooms are good and have a sweet flavor.

Habitat and period of presence: Golden needle mushrooms are found in the leafy woods (especially willows, elms, beeches) on dead wood or strains. They begin to appear from November and persist until spring.

Photo 2.7 : Golden needle mushroom

BLONDE MORELS - *Morchella rotunda*

Description: the **cap** is typically round to slightly oval blonde color. It features deep pockets and wide, well open, sponges-shaped. The **flesh** is tender. The **stipe** is stocky and cylindrical.

Photo 2.8 : Blonde morels

MORELS ARE DELICIOUS and have a strong, fragrant flavor. They are stocky and cylindrical.

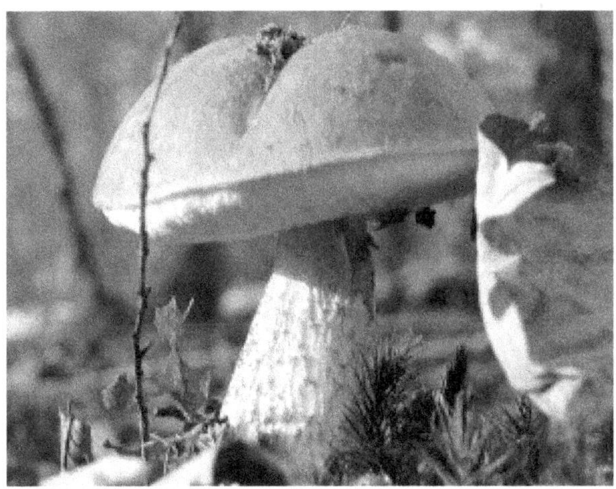 **Habitat and period of presence**: Blondes morels grow in the leafy airy forests of ashes and elms, under the apple trees and on the woods border, under bushes. They start appearing in April and continue until June.

Red-capped scaber stalk - Leccinum aurantiacum

Description: the **cap** is hemispherical and fleshy, orange colored. The margin, slightly round, becomes smooth. The **flesh** is firm, white or pink. It blackens when cut. The **hymenium** has long whitish tubes that turn brown or gray with age. The **stipe** is stocky and rough, whitish or greyish and greening towards its base.

Red-capped scaber stalks are very good and have a sweet flavor.

Photo 2.9 : Red-capped scaber stalk

PLEASE NOTE THESE MUSHROOMS should be cooked (at least 15 minutes), otherwise they can cause stomach pain.

Habitat and period of presence: Red-capped scaber stalks can be found in the poplar forests, hornbeam or birch. They appear from August to November.

Saffron milk cap - *Lactarius deliciosus*

Description: Saffron milk cap is one of the best known members of the large milk-cap genus Lactarius within the Russulales order. The **cap** is convex, flattens and becomes depressed with age, its color is orange-red. It is covered with a whitish waxy layer. The margin is thin and wound. The **flesh** is white to orange, firm and brittle and slowly turns green when cut. It reveals when broken its milk which is abundant and orange. The **hymeniumhas** tight, uneven, orange gills.

The **stipeis** stocky, orange, hollow at the base.

Saffron milk caps are delicious, even if the next mushroom is better ;-) and have a fruity flavor.

Photo 2.10 : Saffron milk cap

HABITAT AND PERIOD of presence: Saffron milk caps are found in coniferous forests, especially with pine trees, and often on the moss. They appear in autumn.

Bloody milk cap - *Lactarius sanguifluus*

Photo 2.11 : Bloody milk cap

DESCRIPTION : Bloody milk cap is maybe the most delicious member of the large milk-cap genus Lactarius in the Russulales order. The **cap** is hemispherical, flattens and becomes depressed with age, gray-ocher nuanced red. The **flesh** is red, firm. It reveals its red scarce milk "blood" when broken. The **hymenium** has tight gills, uneven whitish to red. The **stipe** is stubby.

Bloody milk caps are delicious, better than the saffron milk caps, and have a fruity flavor!

Habitat and period of presence: Bloody milk caps are found in coniferous forests, especially pine and often under the needles fall to the ground. They appear in autumn.

Orange peel fungus - *Aleuria aurantia*

Description: these mushrooms grow often in groups. The **cap** is small and cup-shaped, 2 to 10 cm, yellow or orange. The interior is brightly colored. The **flesh** is thin and fragile, with no particular smell. The **stipe** is almost nonexistent, the fungus resting directly on the floor.

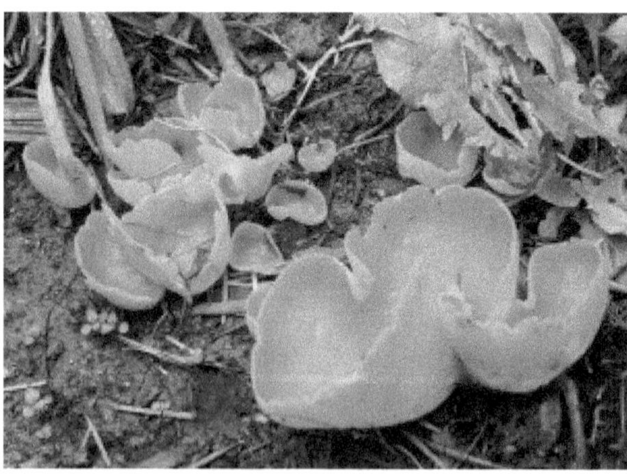

Photo 2.12 : Orange peel fungus

ORANGE PEEL FUNGI ARE good, but do not have a particular taste.

Please note these mushrooms should be cooked (at least 15 minutes), otherwise they can cause digestive disorders.

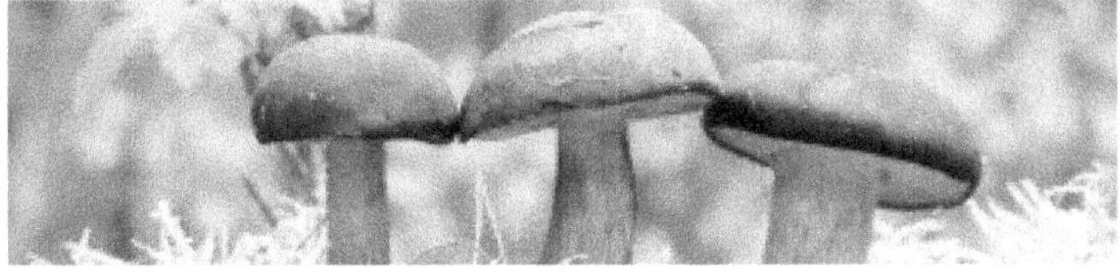

Habitat and period of presence: Orange peel fungi are found in coniferous woods, clearings and wet locations. They appear in autumn and persist until December.

3. White or cream mushrooms

Oyster mushroom - *Pleurotus ostreatus*

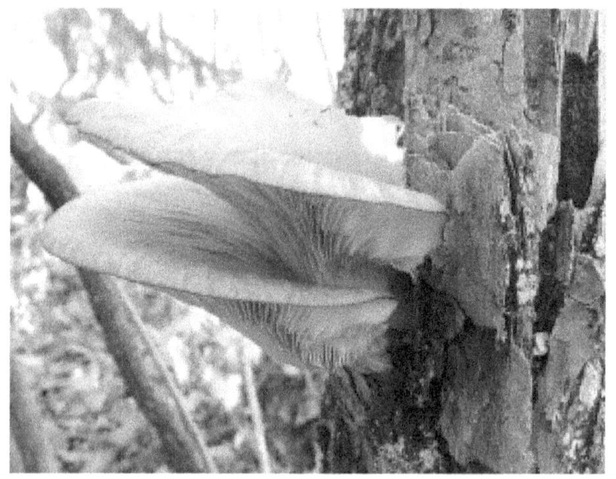

Photo 3.1 : Oyster mushroom

DESCRIPTION: the **cap** is convex and flattens with age. It is eccentric, shell-shaped, of 7 to 14 cm, whitish gray to even blackish. The surface is shiny and smooth with a sinuous margin. The **flesh** is thick and white, becoming soft and elastic with age. The **hymenium** has white gills, tight enough. The **stipe** may be absent or small, white and firm.

Oyster mushrooms are very good with a mild flavor and have a smell of wet linen.

**Habitat and period of presence**: Oyster mushrooms grow on trees or dead leafy woods and begin to appear in autumn and persist until winter. They grow often in large clumps.

King trumpet mushroom - *Pleurotus cornucopiae*

Description: the **cap** widens as a cone or a funnel. It is 4 to 12 cm, whitish to beige. The surface is smooth, presenting a coiled margin. The **flesh** is firm and white, soft and fibrous with age.

The **hymenium** has white gills, a little tight, uneven.

The **stipe** is a bit small, lateral, white and firm.

Photo 3.2 : King trumpet mushroom

KING TRUMPET MUSHROOMS are very good with a mild flavor, a flour odor becoming a little unpleasant with age.

Habitat and period of presence: King trumpet mushrooms grow on living or dead leafy wood and start appearing in spring until summer. They often grow in large clumps and have a welded base.

Trooping funnel or Monk's head - *Infundibulicybe geotropa*

Description: its **cap** is 7 to 20 cm large. When young it is shaped as a keel, then it becomes convex. It becomes flat and hilly, then looks like a widening funnel. Its margin is smooth.

The **flesh** is firm and white. The **hymenium** has thin gills, colored from cream to beige. The **stipe** is long and strong, fibrous at surface, thicker towards the base.

Photo 3.3 : Monk's head

MONK'S HEAD MUSHROOMS are good and have a mild flavor and a smell of cut hay. It is best when young.

Habitat and period of presence: Monk's head mushrooms are found in the woods of well ventilated leafy trees but also in meadows and clearings and often form "fairy rings". They begin to appear from August and continues until November.

St. George's mushroom - *Calocybe gambosa*

Photo 3.4 : St. George's mushroom

DESCRIPTION: the **cap** measures from 3 to 10 cm. It is whitish, dull, fleshy, convex when young and depressing with age. Its margin is coiled and undulated. The **gills** are white, tight and yellow with age. The **flesh** is white and tender.

The **stipe** is short and often eccentric, pinkish to white.

St. George's mushrooms are delicious and have a sweet taste and a strong smell of flour.

Habitat and period of presence: St. George's mushrooms grow in leafy or coniferous woods, usually on the edge, in grassy areas. They begin to appear from August and persist until October.

Be careful not to confuse them with *Clitocybe candicans* or *Clitocybe cerussata* whose smell is less mealy - they are **very toxic**! Another distinction is the margin which is not wavy. If you have any doubt, it is better not to eat mushrooms.

Photo 3.5 : Clitocybe candicans - TOXIC!

GYPSY MUSHROOM - *Cortinarius caperatus*

Photo 3.6 : Gypsy mushroom

DESCRIPTION: This is a gregarious mushroom that grows on siliceous ground, in groups. The **cap** is rounded and flattens with age, wrinkled toward the edge. It is yellow reddish.

The **flesh** is firm, cream to pink, and colors water in yellow.

The **hymenium** consists of highly unequal gills and jagged, rusty brown color. The **stipe** is long, measuring from 8 to 12 cm, cream, widening downwards. It has a ridged ring, membranous and tenacious.

Gypsy mushrooms are very good without having a special flavor.

Habitat and period of presence: Gypsy mushrooms grow in leafy woods (mainly beech) and coniferous (spruces) especially in the mountains. They begin to appear from August and continue until October. They grow in large groups.

Lawyer's wig - Coprinus comatus

Photo 3.7 : Lawyer's wig

DESCRIPTION: This is a gregarious mushroom, recognizable by the cuticle with scales covering the cap and the stipe. The **cap** is fragile taper shaped, from 5 to 15 cm, and opens bell-shaped with age. Its whitish scales becomes gray. The **flesh** is fragile, white then pink and black with age. The **hymenium** has white gills, very tight and colors in pink and black with age.

The **stipe** is long and white smooth when young and with yellowing scales with age.

Lawyer's wigs are very good and have a nice flavor. You need to consume them when they are white and quickly after picking them.

It is possible to conserve them a few days by soaking them in water.

Habitat and period of presence: Lawyer's wigs are found in meadows, clearings, roadsides and even gardens. They begin to appear from May and persist until November.

Horse mushroom - Agaricus arvensis

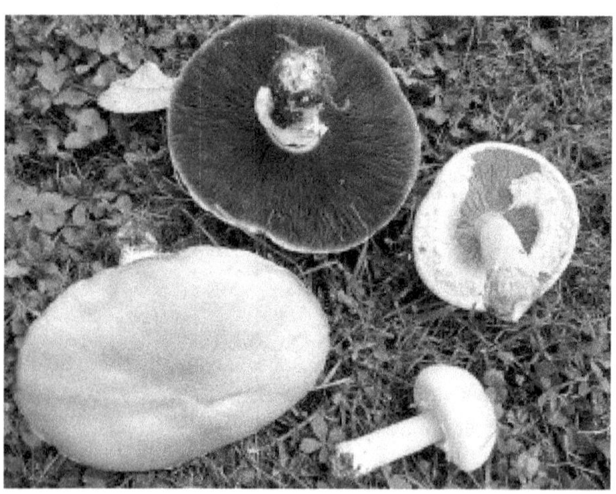

Photo 3.8 : Horse mushroom

DESCRIPTION: the **cap** is hemispherical and has a satin white color. It flattens with age, slightly yellowing and rupturing by sheets. The **flesh** is firm and thick, white colored. The **hymenium** has white, uneven gills, tight and fines.

The **stipe** is robust, 5 to 15 cm long with a ring, whose bottom forms a kind of gear wheel.

Horse mushrooms are delicious, have a sweet flavor and a slightly aniseed odor.

Habitat and period of presence: Horse mushrooms grow in meadows. They start appearing in July and persist until October. They grow singly or in small groups.

Wood mushroom - *Agaricus silvicola*

Description: the **cap** is globular, white, flattens with age and becomes yellow. The **flesh** is thin and whitish. The **hymenium** has cream, uneven, thin and tight gills. They turn red then brown with age. The **stipe** is slender, 5 to 12 cm long, white-gray, with a bulb at the base, with a large and fragile yellow-white ring.

Photo 3.9 : Wood mushroom

WOOD MUSHROOMS ARE delicious and have a sweet flavor, a strong aniseed odor.

Habitat and period of presence: Wood mushrooms grow in leafy woods or conifers. They begin to appear in June and continue until November. They grow singly or in small groups.

Photo 3.10 : Death cap - NOT EDIBLE!!

BE CAREFUL NOT TO CONFUSE them with the deadly **Amanita** including *Amanite phalloïde* which are **very toxic** - its common name is the **Death cap!** A distinction is the volva (a kind of bag) at the base of the stipe, but also the gills which are always white and do not smell as anise. If you have any doubt, it is better not to consume / touch these mushrooms.

Meadow mushroom - *Agaricus campestris*

Description: the **cap** is hemispherical and satin, white, flattening with age, slightly yellowing and covered with small scales. The **flesh** is white and becomes slightly reddish in tbse of bruising. The **hymenium** has pink gills, fine and tight, turning to brown with age. The **stipe** is robust, does not exceed 7 cm long with a thin ring.

Photo 3.11 : Meadow mushroom

MEADOW MUSHROOM ARE delicious and have a mild flavor like the mushroom you find in the supermarket. Its odor is fruity.

Habitat and period of presence: Meadow mushroom grow in prairie grasses and pastures. They begin to appear from May and continue until October. They grow singly or in small groups.

Be careful not to confuse them with the deadly Amanita including ***Amanite phalloïde*** or ***Amanita virosa*** which are **very TOXIC**! Only one mushroom is enough to kill a person. A distinction is the volva (a bag of species) at the base of the foot, the gills always white like the rest of the fungus. If you have any doubt, it is better not to consume / touch mushrooms.

Photo 3.12 : Amanita virosa - TOXIC!!

HEDGEHOG MUSHROOM - *Hydnum repandum*

Photo 3.13 : Hedgehog mushroom

DESCRIPTION: the **cap** is fleshy, bumpy, has a creamy white color. The margin is thick, coiled, and then becomes sinuous and lobed. The **flesh** is thick and firm, brittle and presents a white color that turns orange with age. The **hymenium** has cream spines, long and fragile, that turn brown with age.

The **stipe** is thick, is either white or the same color as the cap, and is sometimes off-center, turning reddish with age.

Hedgehog mushroom are very good and have a sweet flavor.

Habitat and period of presence: Hedgehog mushroom can be found in leafy woods (especially oak) or conifers. They often grow in groups and appear in autumn from September to November.

Parasol mushroom - *Macrolepiota procera*

Photo 3.14 : Parasol mushroom

THE PARASOL MUSHROOM, is a kind of edible mushrooms that I have discovered not so long ago and that I had the opportunity to test before adding it to my little guide :-).

Description: the **cap** is ovoid then convex, then broad, like an umbrella, up to 30 cm in diameter, white-cream color. It has a nipple when it is spread out as an umbrella. The cap is covered with brown scales, denser towards the center. The **flesh** is soft, white with a fruity smell. The **hymenium** has white, tight, soft blades. The **stipe** is long and fine, 15 to 40 cm. It is hollow and bulbous at the base, with a double, whitish and sliding ring. It is fibrous making it difficult to eat, but can be used thinly sliced in soups or sauces.

The parasol mushrooms are very good and have a sweet and delicate flavor. The cap can be fried in oil or barbecued or made in a cream sauce that will give it more flavor. Small tip: the young parasol mushrooms will open their hat if you leave them in a glass for a few days;-).

Habitat and period of presence: The parasol mushrooms have several names depending on the region or country and are found in the clear woods or the glades, or even along the road as I found several. They often grow in groups, but may also be solitary and appear from July to October and even until December in the southern regions. These fungi are found not only in Europe, but also in America, Australia, India, Siberia, the Far East, Japan and even Africa.

Photo 3.15 : False parasol or green-spored parasol **NOT EDIBLE!**

BE CAREFUL NOT TO CONFUSE them with the **false parasol** or **green-spored parasol** in North America (*Chlorophyllum molybdites*) which is toxic - the big difference is their green blades unlike the edible one which has white blades under the cap. In Europe the parasol mushroom can be confused with the ***Lepiota helveola*** which is toxic, but whose height does not exceed 7 cm and its flesh is slightly pink.

4. Other color mushrooms

Charcoal burner - *Russula cyanoxantha*

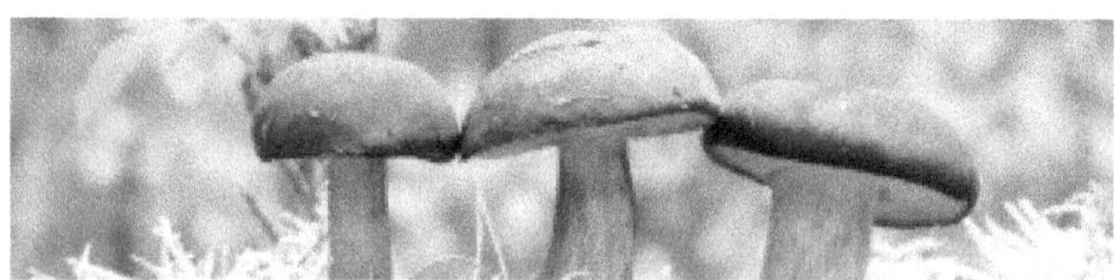

Photo 4.1 : Charcoal burner

DESCRIPTION: the **cap** goes from purple to olive green through gray and its width is often up to 15 cm. The russula often has flexible white gills and do not break under finger pressure.

The **stipe** is white, from 5 to 10 cm tall with a diameter of 2 to 3 cm with the consistency of polystyrene.

Charcoal burners are good and have a slight nutty flavor.

Habitat and period of presence: Charcoal burners are very common in leafy woods and begin to appear from July and persist until October. They often grow in groups under beeches, oaks or birches.

Aniseed toadstool - *Clitocybe odora*

Photo 4.2 : Aniseed toadstool

DESCRIPTION: its **cap** is thin, of 3 to 7 cm, convex and flattened with age, milky greenish blue color. Its margin is smooth and wrapped and rises with age. The **flesh** is firm and elastic, with a pale green color. The **hymenium** has fines and spaced gills, paler than the cap.

The **stipe** is short, fibrous, cylindrical paler than the cap.

Aniseed toadstool are good and have a mild aniseed flavor and a smell of aniseed. They are better when young.

Habitat and period of presence: Aniseed toadstool are found in quite dark sub-hardwood (birch, beech), but also of coniferous trees. They often form circles or colonies. They begin to appear from August and continue until September.

Hen of the woods - *Grifola frondosa*

Description: The fruiting **body** is greyish, forms a mass up to 50 cm in diameter, consisting of many curled caps with wavy margins coming from the ramifications of a very short trunk. This is a fungus that can weigh several kilos! The **flesh** is thick, soft, slightly fibrous, white to cream. The **stipe** is short, whitish.

Photo 4.3 : Hen of the woods

HENS OF THE WOODS ARE good with no particular flavor.

Habitat and period of presence: Hens of the woods can be found at the base of oaks and chestnuts, or on their strains. They begin to appear from August on and continue until November.

Umbrella Polypore - *Polyporus umbellatus*

Description: The fruiting body, whitish grey, forms a mass up to 40 cm in diameter, consisting of many caps depressed umbrella-shaped with a wavy margin. This is a fungus that can weigh several kilos! The **flesh** is meaty, soft, white to cream.

The **stipe** is short, whitish to cream.

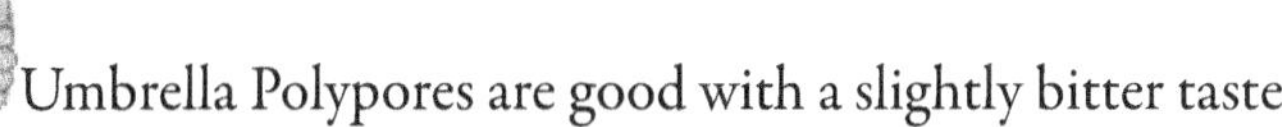 Umbrella Polypores are good with a slightly bitter taste.

Photo 4.4 : Umbrella Polypore

 **HABITAT AND PERIOD of presence**: Umbrella Polypores can be found at the base of leafy trees (oak mostly), or their strains. They start appearing in July and persist until October.

Common morel - *Morchella esculenta*

Description: the **cap** is ovoid, blackish, yellowish and gray. It features deep and wide pockets, and a generally clearer grooves.

The **flesh** is brittle, gray on the cap, and white on the stipe.

The **stipe** is short and stubby, hollow, white or yellowish.

Common morels are delicious and have a sweet flavor.

Habitat and period of presence: Common morels are to be found in the leafy airy forests - ashes, elms, poplars, under apple and other fruit trees in the old fire places and at the edge of the woods, under bushes. They start appearing in April and continue until June.

Photo 4.4 : Common morel

PLEASE NOTE THESE MUSHROOMS should be cooked (at least 15 minutes), otherwise they can cause digestive disorders.

Black morel - *Morchella elata*

 **Description**: the **cap** is conical, thin, elongated, brownish. It features narrow, deep and elongated cells and the grooves are generally darker. The **flesh** is tender and white. The **stipe** usually measures half of the cap. It is hollow, whitish.

Black morels are delicious and have a mild flavor and a fragrant smell.

Please note these mushrooms should be cooked (at least 15 minutes), otherwise they can cause digestive disorders.

Habitat and period of presence: Black morels are found mainly in the mountains, in leafy forests as ashes, elms, and even mixed with Scots pine or spruces not very dense, bordering rivers. They begin to appear in February and continue until May.

Violet chanterelle - *Gomphus clavatus*

Description: The **cap** is a little depressed at the top with a sinuous margin, becoming lobed, white-lilac and yellow-brown. The **flesh** is white, firm. The **hymenium** has weavy gills of purple color, then brown-ocher. The **stipe** is short, often side positioned, thinner at the bottom, purple color that becomes lighter with age.

Violet chanterelles are delicious and have a sweet flavor.

Habitat and period of presence: Violet chanterelle are found in coniferous forests especially in groups. They appear from July to November.

5. Gourmet re cipes

Omelette with chanterelles

A quick and easy recipe to make back from the woods to taste your chanterelles ;-).

- 350 g de chanterelles, 5 eggs, 100 g smoked trout

- a small piece of butter

Wash the mushrooms and cut the feet if earthy. In a frying pan, put some butter and the mushrooms. After 2-3 minutes, add the smoked trout cut into strips and mix. Add the beaten eggs and cover. Turn omelette 3-4 minutes later and leave for another 2 minutes.

Tocanita de ciuperci - **a Romanian specialty**

THIS IS MY FAVORITE dish with mushrooms. It can be done with any type of mushrooms, even with those of Paris. I love this dish with chanterelles, but it is also excellent with boletus. For classical mushrooms or oyster mushrooms it is necessary to add more herbs to raise the taste ;-).

- 800 g mushrooms or more, 1 onion, 3 garlic cloves
- a small piece of butter, herbs, fresh cream

Wash and clean the mushrooms. Cut into slices if you have big mushrooms. In a frying pan, put some butter and the onion finely chopped. Leave two minutes and then add the mushrooms. Let cook for about ten minutes while mixing from time to time. Add finely chopped garlic and herbs. Allow another ten minutes. Serve with fresh cream.

Wood mushrooms pie

- 500 g mushrooms or more
- 2 pastries (puff or shortcrust) or 1 egg+3 tablespoons of fresh cream + 125 g margarine + flour
- 1 small onion, 1/2 tin of pâté or foie gras, 1 or 2 eggs
- Herbs, chopped parsley, salt, pepper

Pastry: The simplest way to do this pie is with a ready made pastry, but otherwise put all the ingredients listed and mix. Add as much flour as necessary, so that the dough is neither too soft, nor too hard, nor sticky. Divide the dough thus made into two parts and spread the first with a rolling pin. Wash and clean mushrooms.

Filling: Finely chop the onion. Blond it with a little oil. Add the mushrooms cut into small pieces. Put salt and pepper according to your taste. Remove from the heat and add the pâté by mixing. Let cool, then add eggs and finely chopped parsley.

In a baking dish or in a pie dish, put the first pastry. If it is puffed, drill it with a fork to avoid swelling during cooking. Spread the filling with the mushrooms and then cover with the second pastry. In a small cup, break an egg and mix the yellow with the white. Using a brush, spread on the dough. Bake in a hot oven for about 30 minutes.

This is a pie that is good to eat hot or cold.

Mushrooms of the woods in béchamel sauce

- 500 g mushrooms or more, some butter, 2 tbs of flour
- 2 tbs oil, 2 tbs fresh cream, salt, pepper

Wash and clean the mushrooms. Cut into slices if big mushrooms.

In a frying pan, put some butter and the mushrooms. Leave to cook for about ten minutes - until the mushrooms have left their sauce.

In a saucepan, mix over the heat, flour with oil until flour blonde. Add gradually the sauce let by the mushrooms and then the fresh cream while mixing. Remove from heat and add mushrooms. Bake for about thirty minutes.

Gratin with mushrooms

- 500 g mushrooms or more, some butter, 1 onion
- 3 garlic cloves, 1 egg, grated cheese, salt, pepper

Wash and clean the mushrooms. Cut into slices if big mushrooms. In a frying pan, put some butter and the onion finely chopped. Leave to blond and then add the mushrooms. Cook for 2 minutes while mixing from time to time. Add finely chopped garlic and herbs and leave 1-2 more minutes. Remove from heat. Let cool a little and then add the eggs. Cover with grated cheese.

Put in a heated oven for about thirty minutes until the cheese is melted and golden.

Moussaka with mushrooms

- 500 g mushrooms or more, some butter, 1 onion
- 3 garlic cloves, 6 - 8 big potatoes, 2 eggs, grated chees
- 3 tbs fresh cream, salt, pepper

Wash and clean the mushrooms. Cut into slices if large mushrooms.

In a frying pan, put some butter and the onion finely chopped. Leave to blond and then add the mushrooms. Cook for 5 minutes while mixing from time to time. Add finely chopped garlic and herbs. Remove from heat. Let cool a little and then add the eggs and the fresh cream. Peel and wash the potatoes. Cut them into thin slices.

In a baking dish, put a layer of potatoes' slices. Then a layer of mushrooms. Then another layer of potatoes ... and so on. Cover with grated cheese. Bake in a hot oven for about forty minutes.

Filled meadow mushrooms

This is a recipe that also works with champignons de Paris. Choose mushrooms with large caps that can be filled like meadow mushrooms.

- A dozen large mushrooms or more, some butter, bacon
- 3 finely chopped garlic cloves, grated cheese, salt, pepper

Wash the mushrooms and remove the feet. On a baking sheet, put the caps on. Finely cut the feet and put a little bit in each cap. Add one or more dices of bacon (depending on the size of the cap). Then some small pieces of garlic. In each cap, put a tiny bit of butter or a few drops of oil, then a little grated cheese.

Bake in a hot oven for about ten minutes. The time of cooking depends on the type of mushrooms, but you will be able to realize when it(s done because the mushrooms will soften a little, the cheese will melt and it will feel super good... ***Bon appétit !***

Gratined mushrooms pancakes

- 200 g mushrooms or more, a dozen of pancakes
- some butte, 1 onion, bacon, 1 tbs fresh cream
- grated chees, pepper

Wash and clean the mushrooms. Cut into small pieces. In a frying pan, put a knob of butter and the onion finely chopped. Leave to blond and then add the mushrooms. Cook for 2 minutes while mixing from time to time. Remove from heat. Let cool a little and then add the fresh cream. Fill the pancakes with this filling and arrange them in a baking dish, oiled beforehand. Cover with grated cheese. Bake in a hot oven for about 15 minutes until the cheese is melted and golden.

Breaded oyster mushrooms

It works with oyster mushrooms, but also with other mushrooms with a fairly flat cap...

- About 20 oyster mushrooms or other flatted cap mushrooms
- an egg, some milk, flour, breadcrumbs, frying oil

Wash the mushrooms. On a sheet of aluminum or waxed paper put a small pile of flour and another with breadcrumbs. In a bowl beat the egg with a little milk. If you have more mushrooms, add another egg and milk. In a frying pan, put the frying oil (mushrooms must bathe completely). Start heating the oil while you pan the mushrooms. For each mushroom do the following : pass it into the flour, then into the egg, again into the flour, finally into the breadcrumbs. Immerse in hot oil. Turn over after 5 minutes when golden brown. Leave for another 3 minutes, then drain on absorbent paper.

Pasta with mushrooms

It is a very fast and succulent dish that can be made with any kind of mushrooms. A great classic of our family that even my son knows how to do and that everyone loves ;-).

- 500 g mushrooms, 500 g pastas, 1 onion, bacon
- olive oil, herbs, 4 tbs fresh cream, grated cheese

Wash and clean the mushrooms. Cut them into slices. Put water to boil for pasta. When you dip the pasta you can start making the mushroom topping. In a frying pan, put the olive oil and the onion finely chopped. Leave to blond and then add the bacon and mushrooms. Leave to cook for about ten minutes while mixing from time to time. Add herbs and pepper (the bacon has already salt!). Add the fresh cream and mix. Leave another 2 minutes. Drain the pastas and put them on the plates. Pour grated cheese and then the mushrooms. **Bon appétit !**

Credits

Thank you to all the kind souls who offer online tools and free resources to use for those who always want to learn and improve!

<u>Photos credits:</u>

Photo 1.1 : By Szabi237 - Own work, CC BY 3.0

Photo 1.2 : Par Tifred25 (Travail personnel), via Wikimedia Commons

Photo 1.3 : Par LitvinovSSderivative work: Ak ccm

Photo 1.4 : By Achim Bollmannderivative work: Ak ccm

Photo 1.5 : By Archenzoderivative work: Ak ccm

Photo 1.6, 3.1,6 : By Jerzy Opioła - {Own}, GFDL

Photo 1.7, 4.2 : By H. Krisp - Own work, CC BY 3.0

Photo 1.8 :By This image was created by user Gerhard Koller (Gerhard) at Mushroom Observer

Photo 1.9, 3.1 : Par Jean-Pol GRANDMONT — Photographie personnelle

Photo 1.10 : Par Pau Cabot — Travail personnel, CC BY-SA 3.0

Photo 1.11, 2.1, 3.10, 4.4 : Par Andreas Kunze — Travail personnel, CC BY-SA 3.0

Photo 1.12 : Par Miika Silfverberg from Vantaa, Finlandderivative work: Ak ccm

Photo 2.3 : By Jason Hollinger - Purple-Tipped Coral Fungus

Photo 2.2 : By böhringer friedrich derivative work: Ak ccm , via Wikimedia Commons

Photo 2.4 : Par Bernie — Travail personnel, Domaine public

Photo 2.5, 3.3,5 : Par Strobilomyces — Travail personnel

Photo 1.13 : Par Jose Luis Cernadas Iglesias (originally posted to Flickr as 879-Agrocybes)

Photo 2.8 : By Pascal Blachier - Flickr

Photo 2.9 : By Tifred25 - Own work, CC BY-SA 3.0

Photo 2.11 : By H. Krisp - Own work, CC BY 3.0

Photo 2.12 : Par 2011-11-15_Aleuria_aurantia_6364528013_ 1a6a132e3e_o.jpg: born1945 from Hillsboro, Oregon, USAderivative work: Ak ccm

Photo 3.5 : Par James Lindsey at Ecology of Commanster

Photo 3.8 : By © Salix / Wikimedia Commons, CC BY-SA 3.0

Photo 3.9 : By Johann Harnisch, CC BY-SA 3.0

Photo 3.10 : Stu's Images, via Wikimedia Commons

Photo 3.13 : By user Alan Rockefeller at Mushroom Observer, a source for mycological images.

Photo 3.15 : Par Nathan Wilson — http://mushroomobserver.org/observer/show_original/538

Photo 4.1 : By Russule_charbonniere.jpg: MediAttaderivative work: Ak ccm

Photo 4.3 : By Lebracderivative work: Ak ccm, CC BY-SA 3.0

Photo 4.5 : This image was created by user Dan Molter (shroomydan) at Mushroom Observer

HOW TO GET THE EBOOK FOR FREE

Did you appreciate this guide? Would you like to have an electronic version of it, for free? You could then enjoy it on your smartphone or tablet, always at your fingertips and more environmentally friendly! It is easy: just write a review on the website where you bought the paper version, and send me an email with a proof of your review and

I will send you the ebook right away, into your inbox! For that, simply use my email address: cristina.rebiere@gmail.com

Hoping to read from you soon ☺

Cristina.

Authors

Cristina & Olivier Rebière met at the age of 17 in Romania, shortly after the fall of the Berlin Wall and the Romanian Revolution of December 1989. After two years of correspondence and several meetings, Cristina was able to get a scholarship to study in France and became Olivier's wife in 1993. Since then, these two "life adventurers" have had an existence full of twists and turns, during which they fell in love with travel, entrepreneurship and writing. Their books are useful, practical, and will fill you up with energy and creativity. In addition to your practical guides of this collection, discover other ebooks on their website **http://www.OlivierRebiere.com**

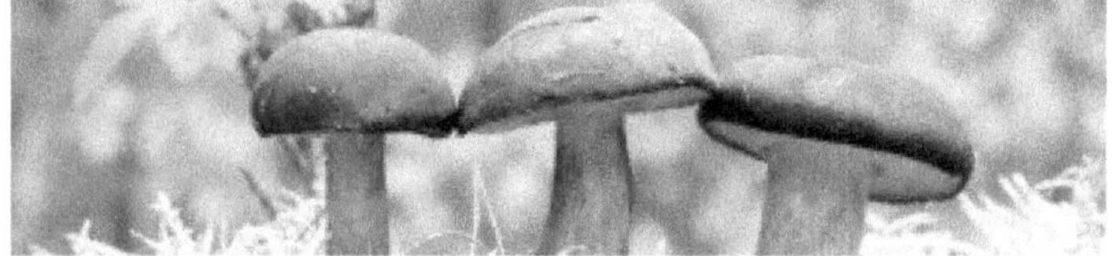

Don't miss out!

Visit the website below and you can sign up to receive emails whenever Cristina Rebiere publishes a new book. There's no charge and no obligation.

https://books2read.com/r/B-A-COEX-HGEHC

BOOKS 2 READ

Connecting independent readers to independent writers.

Did you love *How to Choose Mushrooms*?? Then you should read *Herbal Teas to be in Good Health*[1] by Cristina Rebiere!

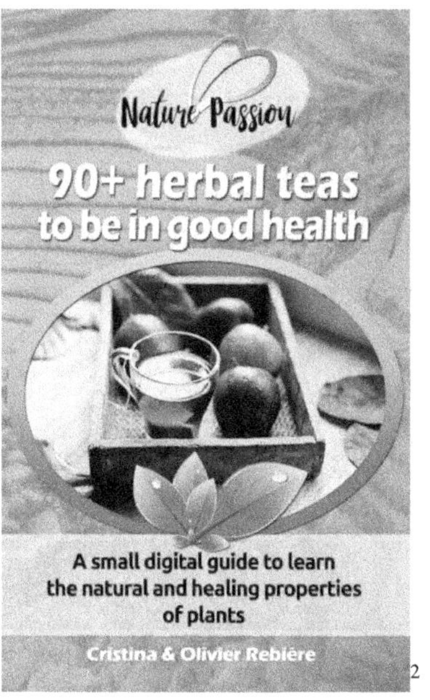

A small digital guide to learn the natural and healing properties of plants

Want a cup of herbal tea for your health?Would you like to know how to use plants and fruits to prepare herbal teas and remain in good health?Life is also made of simple pleasures that can turn into pure happiness easily Our collection of practical ebooks Nature Passion is going to prove it to you!Discover small, easy and cheap books that will help you to bring nature into your life every day!

We have over a decade of experience in breeding small animals and presenting them to children as part of a mini-zoo. We would like to share the knowledge we've gained from our seniors and ancestors. We also love

---

1. https://books2read.com/u/3LNqEe

2. https://books2read.com/u/3LNqEe

to cook and of course love preparing any kind of herbal teas to remain in good health, naturally

We wish to share with you our knowledge and our helpful tips for « tame » simply this Nature from which, sometimes, modern life takes us away...

You are going to discover small useful practical guides, always handy in your smartphone

Herbal teas to be in good health

In this eGuide you are going **to find out all the benefits of fruits, vegetables and other plants**, but also beverages that will strengthen your health!

What are you going to find in this « eGuide *Nature Passion* »?

our tips to prepare your herbal teasmore than 90 recipes, by ailment130+ photos

So, are you ready to bring nature into your everyday life?! Yes?

Let's go!

Kind regards,

Cristina & Olivier Rebiere

Also by Cristina Rebiere

Cathy Merlin
Le monde des elfes
Elves' world
The Path of Secrets
El Sendero de los Secretos
El Mundo de los Elfos

Guide Education
Mastering the Gantt chart
Use Google Forms for Evaluation
Create a Website in One Hour
Motive a su Clase Mediante el Juego
¿Qué es un Diagrama de Gantt?

Heirs of the Stone Age
The Waters' Fury
The Amulet of the Seasons

Kids Experience
Activities & Games for Kids to do Everywhere
Cooking with children

Nature Passion
101 Smoothies for Your Health
Herbal Teas to be in Good Health
90+ Tés de Hierbas Medicinales para su Salud
Cómo Crear un Huerto Orgánico en su Balcón
How to Choose Mushrooms?

Team Building Inside
Team Building Ejercicios "Rompehielos"
Team Building -Trabajo en Equipo y Coordinación
Team Building - Comunicación
Team Building - Gestión de Proyecto y Innovación
Team Building - Estrategia y Planificación

Voyage Experience
Martinique
Zaragoza and Aragon
Timisoara et sa région
Krakow and its Region
Granada - City Trip in Andalusia

Zen Attitude
Cómo salir de una relación tóxica
El arte de la simplicidad
The art of simplicity
Comment sortir d'une relation toxique
Free Yourself from Toxic Relationships
Come Uscire da una Relazione Tossica